CH

DISCARD

D1022111

George S. Patton

George S. Patton

World War II General & Military Innovator

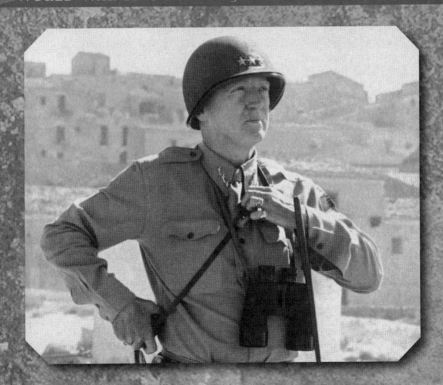

by **Martin Gitlin**

Content Consultant:
Charles Michael Province
Founder, George S. Patton Jr. Historical Society

ABDO
Publishing Company

CREDITS

Published by ABDO Publishing Company, 8000 West 78th Street, Edina, Minnesota 55439. Copyright © 2010 by Abdo Consulting Group, Inc. International copyrights reserved in all countries. No part of this book may be reproduced in any form without written permission from the publisher. The Essential Library™ is a trademark and logo of ABDO Publishing Company.

Printed in the United States of America,
North Mankato, Minnesota
102009
012010

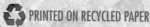 PRINTED ON RECYCLED PAPER

Editor: Holly Saari
Copy Editor: Paula Lewis
Interior Design and Production: Kazuko Collins
Cover Design: Kazuko Collins

Library of Congress Cataloging-in-Publication Data
Gitlin, Marty.
  George S. Patton : World War II general & military innovator / Martin Gitlin.
    p. cm. — (Military heroes)
  Includes bibliographical references and index.
  ISBN 978-1-60453-964-6
  1. Patton, George S. (George Smith), 1885-1945—Juvenile literature. 2. Generals—United States—Biography—Juvenile literature. 3. United States. Army—Biography—Juvenile literature. 4. United States—History, Military—20th century—Juvenile literature. 5. World War, 1939-1945—Campaigns—Juvenile literature. I. Title.

E745.P3G585 2010
355.0092—dc22
[B]
                                        2009032371

TABLE OF CONTENTS

George Smith Patton III served in the U.S. Army in Hawaii in the 1930s.

BROKEN LEG,
DAMAGED SPIRIT

In 1934, Lieutenant Colonel George Smith Patton III was transferred to Hawaii, a territory of the United States. He went to serve as an intelligence officer in the U.S. Army gathering helpful, and sometimes secret, information.

Many would have found such work in a warm, exotic location intriguing, but not Patton. He craved excitement. He yearned for adventure on the battlefield. But Hawaii was at peace—at least for a while. Patton's fiftieth birthday soon came and went. He was so bored that he considered early retirement.

In the late spring of 1937, he accompanied his wife, Beatrice, and their son, George, on an extended vacation at the family's Massachusetts home. In the heat of a July summer day, the couple mounted their horses and began what they hoped to be a relaxing ride. But Beatrice's horse suddenly bolted and bucked. Patton was riding too close to her horse, and it kicked his leg with great force. Patton fell to the ground and passed out. His mind began to explore wild thoughts. He dreamed he had been injured in battle centuries earlier. In his dream, he was escorted to Valhalla, a legendary hall from Norse mythology where heroes killed in battle are received.

No Advancement

One reason why Patton was disenchanted with his role in the military in the late 1930s was his lack of advancement. He applied several times for a job at the U.S. Army Military Academy at West Point, New York. He wanted to help train cadets into being future officers, but he was routinely passed over.

After one rejection, he told of his frustrations to General John J. Pershing, who had served in World War I: "I have gained the impression that possibly the fact that I am very outspoken is held against me in some quarters. . . . Possibly the [honesty] of a fighting soldier is not too well received in peace."[1]

Patton later described the strange fantasy to his nephew, Fred Ayer Jr.:

> *I was lying on some battlefield on a big Norse shield. After a while two armored Vikings came and started to lift me up on that shield to carry me to Valhalla. Then one of them shook his head, and they gently put me down again, and I came to. . . . I guess they're not ready to take me yet. I still have a job to do.*[2]

In just a few years, the significance of Patton's dream would be realized: he would find the job he was meant to do.

Buying Horses

One of Patton's duties in Hawaii was to purchase horses for the army. His love for the animals made this a responsibility he enjoyed. He frequently took his family along on buying expeditions.

BAD NEWS FROM THE X-RAYS

Patton suffered multiple fractures from his accident. The doctor who treated him feared that his leg could be permanently damaged due to the breaks and the severe swelling that resulted. Patton was forced to remain in the hospital for three and one-half months. During that time, he developed a blood clot condition called phlebitis, which almost killed him.

After a horse kicked him in the leg, Patton was hospitalized for three and one-half months.

As he lay on his bed recovering from the accident, Patton had plenty of time to reflect on the past and consider the future. It did not seem to matter in what capacity Patton worked—he was often praised for his performance. Brigadier General Daniel Van Voorhis, who served as chief of staff of the Hawaiian Department, had called Patton "ambitious, progressive, original, professionally studious, conscientious in the performance of his duties [and] the most physically active officer I have ever known."[3]

Patton had gained quite a different reputation in his personal relationships with superior officers and others. He had become known as a stubborn man with a gruff exterior. Yet, Patton had a keen grasp of international politics and military strategy. Both attributes would come in handy as war clouds gathered over Europe and Asia.

THE FUTURE OF WAR

The threat of the United States being pulled into the escalating conflict in Europe energized Patton. Although the United States had

A Legendary Temper

Patton was known for having a temper and using coarse language. A case in point occurred at the 1936 Inter-Island Polo Championship in Hawaii. During a match, Patton collided with Walter Dillingham, a local manufacturer who was very wealthy. Dillingham was captain of the team representing the island of Oahu.

Patton cursed at Dillingham and threatened him. Patton also had used offensive language in front of women at the game, which was considered especially bad-mannered in the 1930s. Commanding General Hugh Drum quickly removed Patton as captain of the Maui island team.

Dillingham, however, insisted that Patton be reinstated. He threatened to remove his team from the field if Patton was not allowed to return to the match.

The incident did not affect Patton's relationship with Dillingham. The two had been close friends on and off the polo field for more than a decade, and they remained so after the confrontation. From then on, General Drum disliked Patton, although their relationship remained civil.

just begun to emerge from the Great Depression in 1937, its leaders were awakening to the possibility of another world war. They feared, however, that it would be far more severe than World War I, which had been limited to Europe.

Though he still felt a love for the cavalry, which fought battles on horseback, Patton believed strongly that the future of ground warfare would be dominated by mechanized weaponry such as tanks. The U.S. Congress, however, was unwilling to appropriate the money necessary to build a large mechanized force.

Patton's thinking may have been ahead of his time in the United States, but in Germany, his thinking was common. In the mid-1930s, the Germans began to build tanks that were faster and stronger than anything previously imagined. They were planning to put them to use in battle. Because he felt that tanks were the future of warfare, Patton refused to sit idly by. He experimented with improved radio communication systems between tanks and helped invent a tank mount for cannons and machine guns.

Patton's most prophetic moment occurred in April 1935, when he warned that Hawaii was highly vulnerable to an attack by the island nation of

Japan. He researched the possible strategies that might be used by Japan and determined that Hawaii could be a target of a surprise strike. He warned that precautions needed to be taken. They included providing ground troops, air forces, ammunition, and an alarm system that would alert soldiers of a Japanese invasion. Patton wrote, "It is the duty of the military to foresee and prepare against the worst possible eventuality."[4]

Six years later, on December 7, 1941, Japan bombed Pearl Harbor, Hawaii. The United States was drawn into the bloodiest war in history—World War II. Little did anyone imagine at that time the great role Patton would play in saving the world from those who sought to conquer it.

But then, he seemed to have been destined for military heroism since the day he was born. —

A Changing Continent

When Fred Ayer Jr. informed his uncle that he was going to visit Europe in 1937, Patton gave him some good advice. He told him to take in as much as possible about the continent because it was not going to stay the same for long. He told Ayer, "Stay as long as you can. See as much as possible because there is going to be one hell of a war—and they're going to blow all kinds of places off the map."[5] Patton was right. World War II began two years later.

Pearl Harbor was attacked six years after Patton warned it was possible.

George's ancestor Hugh Mercer fought and died in the Revolutionary War.

A Young Soldier

While Patton was certainly the best-known warrior to come out of his family, he was not the first. His ancestry boasted many men who had distinguished themselves during times of war.

Among them was Hugh Mercer, a doctor by trade whose close friendship with George Washington had helped earn him the rank of brigadier general in the Continental army. He died a hero's death during the Revolutionary War. Seven of Mercer's grandsons fought for the South during the Civil War, including three who studied at the Virginia Military Institute under General Thomas "Stonewall" Jackson of the Confederate army.

George Smith Patton III was born in San Gabriel, California, on November 11, 1885. In 1887, his sister, Anne, was born. As young children, George and Anne became keenly aware of their family's military background. "Georgie," as his family called him, believed that his ancestors who had died on the battlefield were watching him from heaven. He vowed that he would always live up to their legacies. As a child, he wrote, "men

Patton's Perseverance

Ignacio Callahan was one of Patton's closest friends while growing up. The two boys were highly competitive, but Callahan later admitted that his friend George was better than him in all activities except boxing. He also recalled Patton's perseverance: "When we were about 8 or 10 years old and learning to ride [a horse], Georgie would not be defeated. If a horse threw him, he'd get up and try again."[1]

of my blood . . . have ever inspired me" and "should I falter, I will have disgraced my blood."[2]

The Patton legacy was also marked by wealth. George's father, George Patton II, practiced law with a prestigious California firm. George's mother, Ruth, was the daughter of Benjamin Davis Wilson, one of the state's founding fathers. Wilson was a colorful figure who had worked as a justice of the peace, a politician, and a beaver hunter and trapper. He was also one of California's richest landowners. "Don Benito" Wilson, as he was known, started the citrus industry in California. The state's Mount Wilson is named after him.

Though Wilson died seven years before George was born, his grandson inherited his sense of adventure. But that spirit was not matched by an ability to learn. George likely suffered from dyslexia, a disorder that made it difficult for him to read, write, and spell. He probably also suffered from what is known today as attention deficit disorder, which hinders concentration.

The result was that young George felt pangs of inferiority. He constantly fell behind in his studies. His father hired tutors, and he also read books to his son, mostly of poetry and stories about famous

George, left, with his mother and sister in 1892

warriors. Young George learned about legendary conquerors such as Alexander the Great and Napoleon, as well as General "Stonewall" Jackson and General Robert E. Lee of the Confederacy.

BIRTH OF A DREAM

By the time George was five years old, he had decided that he would be not only a soldier, but also a combat commander. This conviction deepened as time passed. Though life in the military would not grant him the wealth that the Patton family had grown to enjoy, he did not feel that he had any choice. As he later explained,

> *It is as natural for me to be a soldier as it is to breathe and would be as hard to give up all thought of it as it would to stop breathing.*[3]

George continued to struggle in school. At the age of 11, he could not read or write. His father enrolled him at the Classical School for Boys in Pasadena, California. He continued to do poorly in math, reading, and spelling and was ridiculed by his classmates. The taunts and laughter, however, simply motivated him to try harder. He eventually

George Patton II

George Patton II was involved in California politics. He was a Democratic Party nominee for a seat in Congress in 1894. Patton was considered a champion of the common man and railed against the wealthy industrialists of the time such as John D. Rockefeller and Andrew Carnegie, both of whom were worth at least $500 million.

Although he was a proponent for those less privileged, Patton strongly opposed the suffrage movement, which fought for the right of women to vote. Patton was among the leaders of the Men's League Opposed to Suffrage Extension of Los Angeles.

Los Angeles Judge Henry C. Dillon, who campaigned for Patton in 1894, could imagine "the handsome Mr. Patton [standing] in front of the ballot box, swinging the club of brute force over the heads of the women who want to vote."[4]

gained confidence and a sense of
happiness. At home, he was taught
fencing, horseback riding, and
proper manners.

Learning etiquette certainly came
in handy in 1902, when George
met Beatrice Banning Ayer during a
family vacation on Catalina Island.
Beatrice was the petite and highly
refined daughter of wealthy Boston
industrialist Frederick Ayer Sr. She
had been educated in the finest
European schools. During the trip,
George and Beatrice performed
together in a play, in which Beatrice
landed the lead role. George became
infatuated with the young star.

Even so, George was far more
interested in becoming a soldier
than he was in having a girlfriend.
At 17, he informed his father that
he was ready to join the army, but
he was told that there would be no
low-ranking soldiers in the Patton
family. Instead, his father wanted

Pistol Mishap

It did not take long for
George to develop a pas-
sion for weaponry. He
had his own pistol by the
age of five. Once when
he was playing with it in
his grandmother's room,
the weapon accidentally
went off. Fortunately, the
bullet merely nicked him
and burned his finger.

to send George to the U.S. Military Academy at West Point in New York for training to become an officer.

Only One Problem

There was, however, one setback. George, who still struggled with writing, needed to pass a written test to qualify for West Point. His father hoped to sidestep the process by trying to convince California Senator Thomas Bard to appoint George to West Point. But the senator replied that George had to pass the test. So George was sent to the Virginia Military Institute (VMI) in Lexington, Virginia, for one year before taking the test for acceptance at West Point.

The thought of leaving his family and moving more than 3,000 miles (4,828 km) away frightened George. He was also worried that he could not survive the rigorous academic requirements at VMI. Although his

Horseback Riding

George was a very good horseback rider during his childhood. His father had planned to buy him a horse when he was just two years old, but his mother felt that was too young. George received his first horse at the age of four and began taking riding lessons from his uncle and father. By his early teenage years, George was an expert rider.

George, right, at age 16 standing with his father

father had always attempted to instill courage in his son, George worried that he was not brave enough to be a soldier. When his father dropped him off at the military school, George felt scared and alone.

His fear deepened when he discovered that as a cadet he would not be allowed to leave the grounds. Even a visit back home was out of the question. George later wrote, "I never felt lower in my life."[5]

Meanwhile, George's father was busy persuading his friends in the political world to send Senator Bard letters urging George's appointment to West Point. One of the letters came from Los Angeles Judge Henry T. Lee, a former Union officer during the Civil War. Lee wrote a glowing recommendation:

> [George] is a well bred and a well brought up young fellow . . . [who] has developed a great taste and aptitude for the study of military history and the sciences. . . . If blood counts for anything, he certainly comes of fighting stock.[6]

George would certainly live up to those words— but not until he shed the fear of being away from home for the first time.

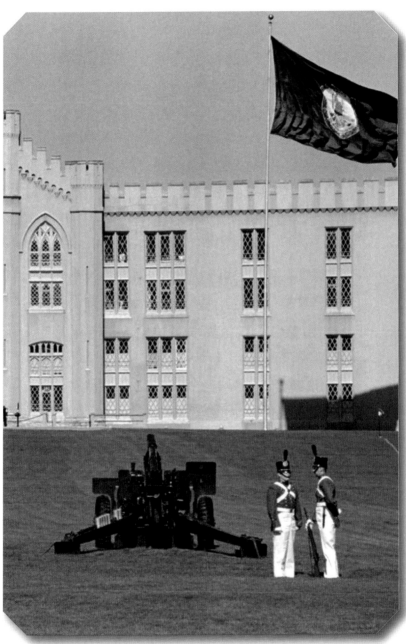

George began attending Virginia Military Institute in 1903.

George Smith Patton III in his 1904 Virginia Military Institute portrait

SCHOOL AND LOVE

fter his arrival at VMI, George Smith
Patton III began to blossom into a fine
student. After an outbreak of typhoid closed the
school for several weeks, he returned to place first
in his class of 93 in algebra, second in both English

and history, and sixth in drawing. He ranked tenth in Latin, a subject with which he had previously struggled.

But VMI was not his school of choice. Patton yearned to attend West Point. His father remained in touch with Senator Bard, who, in early 1904, selected a commission to examine the candidates. The test, however, was to be taken in Los Angeles. Patton had to take a month off from school and travel for six days to take the test.

But the trip was worth it. Patton earned the highest score, clinching his place at West Point. His father could hardly control his joy as he wrote his son a letter of congratulations:

> *You cannot know how proud we feel—and how gratified that you have won your first promotion in the battle of life. If you keep your head level . . . you may look forward to an honorable career—as a soldier of your country. . . . You have in you good soldier blood.[1]*

Patton felt his father's words were true. As a "plebe" (the term for new cadets) at West Point, he compared himself to his fellow classmates. He came to believe that many of them lacked the discipline, drive, and dedication that he held in abundance.

Back to the Drawing Board

Patton's feeling of superiority did not last long, however. The academic struggles that had haunted him in his early years returned. He was frustrated that his grades remained mediocre despite his strong study habits. A young man of tremendous pride, Patton allowed his failures to hurt his confidence.

Not only did he question his future as a student, he now lost his faith in his future as a soldier. He expressed his feelings in a letter to his father:

Academic and Military Success

A cadet's average grades did not rule out military success. At least two classmates who finished lower than Patton also went on to brilliant military careers.

Robert Eichelberger placed sixty-eighth in Patton's class and eventually became one of the most accomplished U.S. generals of World War II. William H. Simpson ranked third from the bottom, but went on to command the Ninth Army in Europe during that same war.

I have always thought that I was a military genius or at least that I was or would be a great general. . . . [But] I see little in which to base such a belief. I am neither quicker nor brighter in any respect than other men, nor do they look upon me as a leader.[2]

During this time, Patton's relationship with Beatrice grew. The two attended the inauguration ball of newly elected President Theodore Roosevelt in March 1905. As they danced through the night, Patton began to fall in love.

His feelings for the young woman did not help his grades, however. He failed both math and French, and he came close to being forced out of West Point. His superiors, however, appreciated his drive to succeed and his performance during drills. They gave him permission to repeat his first year. Rather than scold their son for his academic struggles, his parents provided both support and a special tutor. Patton returned to school the next year determined to succeed.

That is exactly what he did. Although he would never shine as a scholar at West Point, he performed well enough to graduate, even if it would take five years instead of four. He also played football and excelled in both track and fencing.

GAINING RESPECT

Patton's passionate desire and ability to lead a platoon allowed him to blossom. He took over an entire battalion during summer camp after his

Patton the Athlete

Patton was known for his toughness not only in leading men at West Point but also in sports. He played so hard in football that he broke both arms, dislocated his shoulder, and broke his nose three times.

Patton displayed more talent in track. During the West Point Field Day competition in 1908, he won the 120-yard (110-m) hurdles and set a school record in the 220-yard (201-m) hurdles. He also placed second in the 220-yard (201-m) dash.

Reckless Bravery

In his desire to show himself as a leader, Patton sometimes straddled the line between being courageous and being reckless. One example occurred during a drill on the rifle range in his third year at West Point. He suddenly decided to test himself to see if he had the guts to face enemy fire in combat. He emerged from the safety of a trench and stood in front of his fellow cadets as they fired their guns. Patton later claimed proudly that he had been unafraid.

second year. It was then that he learned a valuable lesson. Though he drilled his cadets perfectly, Patton was so demanding and critical that they grew to despise him. The West Point officers promptly demoted him from second to sixth corporal. From this experience, he learned the importance of praise as well as criticism in leading troops.

Patton was soon promoted again to second corporal, then to cadet sergeant major during his junior year. He performed so well that he was given the honor of leading his class as the cadet adjutant during his final year of school.

Patton's life seemed to be on track. Not only was his military education on a good course, his relationship with Beatrice continued to develop. In 1908, Patton spent his Christmas vacation with the Ayers at their family mansion in Boston. He finally found the courage to declare his love for Beatrice, although he was horrified that she might not return his feelings. She, however, replied that she did love him. Patton did not propose then, however, as he wanted to start his career before committing to marriage.

Patton had yet to decide what branch of the service he wanted to join. Though he agonized over the decision, there seemed to be little doubt as to where he was best suited. Patton loved horses, and he was a gifted rider. He also loved action, so the cavalry was a natural choice for him. After graduating on June 11, 1909, he became a second lieutenant in the cavalry. He ended his final year at West Point forty-sixth out of 103 fellow classmen.

Another Courtship

Beatrice Ayer was the woman Patton would marry, but she was not his only love interest. While at West Point, he met an attractive young woman named Kate Fowler, who was a student at Vassar College. Fowler was the daughter of a wealthy business owner who had died several years earlier and left her an estimated $40 million. Patton accompanied the blonde-haired, blue-eyed beauty to a football game at Yale University and even began to consider her as a future bride, though he was still courting Beatrice at the time.

He never hid his interest in Kate from his parents nor even from Beatrice. He admitted in a letter to his father that his proposal to Beatrice was illogical because she did not like war. Kate's wealth was also an important consideration to him.

By early 1910, however, it had become clear that Beatrice would be his wife. Kate and eventual husband Van Merle-Smith later became friends with the Pattons. Their son, Major Van S. Merle-Smith Jr., became an aide to Patton during World War II.

Father of the Bride

One man Patton needed to convince of his good intentions was Beatrice's father, Frederick Ayer. The wealthy textile merchant initially did not want his daughter tied down to an army officer for the rest of her life. But when Patton wrote him a thoughtful letter explaining his passion for the military, Ayer softened. He later grew close to and respectful of his son-in-law.

Before reporting to his cavalry base at Fort Sheridan, Illinois, Patton spent the summer of 1909 attending parties and sailing off the shores of Boston with Beatrice and her family. But the enjoyment of sharing the wealth of the Ayer family would end when he arrived at his drab army surroundings. In a letter to Beatrice, he described his quarters, which featured one desk and an iron bed, as "empty and very dirty."[3]

Beatrice questioned whether she was suited to the life of an army wife. But after Patton's proposal in 1909, she agreed to marry the man who would become one of the greatest military leaders in U.S. history.

Patton at West Point in 1909

Patton at Fort Sheridan, Illinois, in 1910

FIRST TASTES
OF BATTLE

The dream of glory on the battlefield gave way to stark reality for Second Lieutenant Patton. His quarters were drab and damp. No looming conflict offered him the opportunity to live out his dream of becoming a war hero.

The beginning of his military career was not what Patton had thought it would be.

One dream did come true, however. He married Beatrice in a highly publicized ceremony on May 26, 1910, at St. John's Church in Massachusetts. One month later, the elegance of their wedding seemed a distant dream. At Fort Sheridan, the couple lamented the conditions of their shabby room.

Patton was determined to make the most of his experience. He played football and wrote papers about his philosophies on warfare, which were centered on aggressive attack. Although he was an advocate of mechanized weaponry, he showed that he valued soldiers more highly than machines: "We children of a mechanical age are interested and impressed by machines to such an extent that we forget that no machine is better than its operator."[1]

U.S. Army Ranks

The U.S. Army has several ranks of officers. From highest to lowest, they are:
- General of the Army
- General
- Lieutenant General
- Major General
- Brigadier General
- Colonel
- Lieutenant Colonel
- Major
- Captain
- First Lieutenant
- Second Lieutenant

Patton in 1911

Patton's time at Fort Sheridan proved uneventful. He soon arranged a transfer to Fort Myer, Virginia, where he arrived in December 1911. There, Patton began training for the 1912 Summer Olympic Games in Stockholm, Sweden. At the Olympics, the 26-year-old displayed his athletic versatility. He placed fifth among 47 competitors in the modern pentathlon, which consists of fencing, riding, swimming, running, and pistol shooting.

After the Olympic Games, Patton and his family toured Europe. In August 1912, Patton and Beatrice visited Saumur, France, where he took fencing lessons at the prestigious French Cavalry School. Upon his return to the United States, Patton was reassigned to Fort Riley in Kansas. He rewrote the U.S. Army manual on saber fencing and earned the title "Master of the Sword."

By that time, he had become a father. Daughter Beatrice Jr. was born in early 1911. Patton graduated from cavalry school and remained in Fort Riley to become an instructor. In 1915, the family grew again with the birth of the Pattons' second daughter, Ruth Ellen.

Pursuing Pancho Villa

When Patton was transferred to Fort Bliss, Texas, he encountered his first dangerous assignment. Mexican Francisco "Pancho" Villa and his fellow rebels had begun a series of raids across the U.S. border, terrorizing residents of Texas, Arizona,

Patton with his wife, Beatrice, and his daughters, Beatrice Jr., right, and Ruth Ellen, left, in 1919

and New Mexico. After Villa and his gang killed 18 people in Columbus, New Mexico, in March 1916, President Woodrow Wilson called upon the army to track them down.

Brigadier General John J. Pershing, who would later command U.S. troops in World War I, led the expedition. Patton, who was itching for action, pestered Pershing into allowing him to accompany

the group as an aide and an advance
scout for the 10,000-man force.

Patton was not disappointed.
During the search, he spotted Villa's
bodyguard and another Mexican
outlaw in a house at a place called the
Rubio Ranch. Both outlaws began
to fire at Patton and his men from
inside the house. Patton and his men
returned fire and killed both of the
bandits. Patton used the opportunity
to carve two notches in his newly purchased Colt .45
revolver. He would carry the same ivory-handled gun
to war with him later.

The U.S. soldiers in Pershing's force did not
find Villa himself, but they broke up his gang and
ended the border terror. After the mission, Pershing
praised the young man who had begged to join the
fray: "We have a bandit in our ranks. This Patton
boy! He's a real fighter!"[2]

Fighting Again

While Patton was pursuing Villa in Mexico,
the nations of Europe were fighting a war that the
United States had yet to enter. But in April 1917,

Near-death Experience

Patton nearly met his end in Mexico in early October 1916. While he sat in his tent writing a report about his mission, a gasoline-fed lamp exploded and sent flames across Patton's face and hair. He was fortunate. Although the burns were painful, his eyesight was not damaged, and the burns left no scars.

President Wilson committed U.S. troops to World War I. Pershing was appointed to command the forces. Pershing selected Patton, who had been promoted to the rank of captain, to be his aide.

Patton was soon in France, but he was not happy. He had not dreamed of being a soldier his entire life just to perform administrative duties. He craved excitement. He asked Pershing for a transfer to a fighting unit, and the request was granted. Pershing assigned Patton to train, organize,

Tank Warfare

Patton's decision to join the new American Tank Corps was based on the results of the earlier tank battles. The introduction of tanks by the British in the Somme offensive of 1916 produced shock but little results. In the Battle of Flanders a year later, the mud and rugged land prevented British tanks from making an impact. But at Cambria in November 1917, nearly 400 British tanks cut through German defenses. The tanks broke through enemy lines and opened up a gap through which soldiers could advance. However, the British infantry could not keep up.

Patton believed only tactical errors by the British kept the operation from being a success. He felt that tanks were the future of warfare. He was beginning to see the similarities between the tank and the horse. Patton would soon begin to treat tanks like a branch of the cavalry. He wrote to his father-in-law, Frederick Ayer, who replied with some worthy advice:

I know nothing of war. But my advice to you would be to choose the weapon with which you believe can inflict the most punishment on the enemy while at the same time suffering the fewest casualties yourself.[3]

Patton believed that weapon was the tank. He joined the tank corps soon thereafter.

and command the new American Tank Corps.

The task was enormous. Tank warfare had been introduced by the British only one year earlier. The U.S. Army boasted just a few cars and trucks. The tanks would be acquired from the British or French. Patton understood that if tank warfare failed, his reputation and future as an officer could be ruined. While he had strongly advocated the benefits of tank warfare, tanks at the time were primitive and unreliable—their usefulness in battle was questionable.

Patton took a crash course at a French tank school and was promoted to lieutenant colonel in 1918. He worried that the war would end before he had a chance to test his mettle and fighting skills or those of his men. But in August, his brigade received 144 French "Renault" tanks for battle at the Saint-Mihiel salient, a bulge in the German offensive

Growth of the U.S. Army

The U.S. Army expanded once the United States entered World War I. In 1916, two years after the war had begun in Europe, the U.S. Army totaled just 133,000 men. With men drafted into the army and volunteers enlisting, that number jumped to 4.5 million by the time the war ended in November 1918. Approximately 2 million soldiers fought in Europe under the command of General Pershing.

lines. The day before the operation began, Patton rallied his troops:

> You are the first American tanks [in combat]. You must establish the fact that American tanks do not surrender. . . . As long as one tank is able to move it must go forward. Its presence will save the lives of hundreds of infantry and kill many Germans. . . . This our big chance; what we have worked for . . . make it worthwhile.[4]

This was Patton's big chance as well. And he would definitely make it worthwhile.

General Pershing led the pursuit of Pancho Villa in Mexico.

U.S. troops resting near Saint-Mihiel in France during World War I

COMBAT IN
WORLD WAR I

The sun was just rising on September 12, 1918. More than one-half million U.S. soldiers, supported by 110,000 French troops, were preparing to begin an operation against the Germans at the Saint-Mihiel salient in France.

The objective of the French troops was to keep the Germans occupied from the west while U.S. troops attacked from the north and east. Thanks greatly to Patton, some U.S. troops would attack by tank.

French and U.S. troops began the attack with four hours of artillery fire against the Germans. Lieutenant Colonel Patton was unlike other commanders who stayed far away from danger in rear command headquarters during an attack. As a frontline commander, he demonstrated great courage that would earn him the respect of his men.

Patton first watched the movement of his troops from a hillside. But when some of the tanks became bogged down in the mud, Patton walked two miles (3.2 km) to help them. Afterward, rather than return to his safe post, he remained with his men as they pressed forward. He led them from the front while enemy shells burst all around him. The silver oak-leaf emblems on his shoulder straps indicating his rank made him a desirable target for the enemy, but he refused to remove them. He wanted to show his troops that he was not afraid to be in harm's way.

Patton led his troops to the French village of Essey. After a German bombardment, a French soldier suggested turning the tanks back, but Patton

Tanks became an important component of warfare during World War I.

ordered that they continue ahead. He led them
across the bridge into Essey, even though he knew it
could be rigged with explosives.

After Essey, the troops continued toward the next
village of Pannes. They were forced to stop—but not
because of cowardice. All but one of Patton's tanks
ran out of gas.

On the Move Again

Once the tanks had been refueled, they moved forward with the infantry. Once again, Patton walked with the tanks as they continued their attack. They were able to take the village of Pannes from the Germans. Overall, that first day of the attack resulted in the loss of two tanks to artillery fire and five more to engine failure or torn tracks. However, U.S. troops had taken at least 15,000 German prisoners and wiped out enemy control of the Saint-Mihiel salient for the first time in four years.

The success of his initial taste of command in battle left Patton keen for more. He worried that the war would end before he could be given another chance to prove his leadership capabilities, but his fears were unfounded. After Patton's success at Saint-Mihiel, Pershing sent him a letter of congratulations. Pershing also prompted Colonel

Meeting of Future Generals

While under constant shelling in his first battle of the war, Patton met up with U.S. Brigadier General Douglas MacArthur. The two spoke for a while as the fire intensified. Patton admitted that neither could listen to what the other was saying because the shelling was so disconcerting.

Patton and MacArthur would both become prominent U.S. generals in World War II. Patton commanded forces against Germany and Italy in North Africa, Sicily, and Europe. MacArthur did the same against Japan in Asia.

Samuel Rockenbach to assign Patton to lead another tank charge. Rockenbach had been upset that Patton left his observation post to follow his men into battle, but he certainly could not argue with the results.

Patton planned an aggressive attack: 140 tanks would roll over rough terrain through heavily defended German lines. Again, an artillery bombardment softened up the German defenses. And once again, Patton ignored Rockenbach's order to stay at his post. He followed the sounds of gunfire and was pleased to find that his soldiers had advanced five miles (8 km).

But Patton experienced some difficulties. When a number of his men turned back

Cost of Success

Though Patton greatly reduced the German lines at Saint-Mihiel, the price of victory was heavy. An estimated 7,000 U.S. soldiers were either killed or wounded in the operation. And one of them was Patton himself, who refused to watch the battles from afar. He admitted that General Rockenbach "gave me hell for moving forward with my men." However, as he wrote to his wife, Beatrice, he would not have had it any other way: "It had to be done. At least I will not sit in a dug out and have my men out in the fighting."[1]

A lack of communications between tank drivers and their superiors during the war prevented Patton from giving necessary orders during battle. Most likely, this led to unnecessary deaths. That problem would eventually be eliminated with better technology. In future wars, especially World War II, radio communication was used to keep commanders in contact with their troops.

under heavy enemy fire, he rounded them up and gave them a stern talk. The advance continued, but Patton noticed several tanks stuck in trenches. The troops responsible for freeing the tanks were not doing their jobs because they, too, were running away when a shell hit or machine gunfire strafed the area.

Patton would not tolerate cowardice. While bullets flew by him, he ordered a group of men to stay by his side while he personally retrieved shovels from the tanks. He gave the shovels to his men and told them to start digging. When one soldier complained, he struck him over his helmeted head with a shovel. The tanks were soon freed, and Patton was again leading the charge in a barrage of enemy fire.

U.S. Troops' Contributions

Marshal Ferdinand Foch was among the many heroes of World War I. Foch, a Frenchman, was the supreme commander of the Allied forces. In September 1918, Foch assigned General Pershing's First Army the task of reducing the Saint-Mihiel salient. Though Foch's French 505th Tank Brigade aided the operation, it was the U.S. troops, with 16 infantry divisions, who delivered victory and hastened an end to the war.

SCARED BUT ADVANCING

Patton admitted later that he was frightened and believed that his time

*An ambulance arriving to aid wounded soldiers
in France during World War I*

to die had come. But he controlled his feelings and
appeared calm while he continued the advance.

He did not get far, though. A bullet hit him in
the front of his left thigh, went through his leg, and
exited at his rear. Patton continued to walk for about
40 feet (12 m) before collapsing. Patton's orderly,

Joseph T. Angelo, was able to drag
the lieutenant colonel into a nearby
shell hole and apply a bandage to the
bleeding wound. Despite the wound,
Patton continued to give commands.
He ordered Angelo to point out
more targets for the tanks. Patton
was forced to wait an hour before
the shooting calmed down. Then a
stretcher took him to an ambulance
that transported him two miles
(3 km) to the hospital.

Patton's courage and performance
prompted Rockenbach to promote
him to full colonel in October 1918.
When Patton was healed enough to
walk, he sneaked out of the hospital
to return to his tank corps. That
November 11—Patton's birthday—the
war ended. To many people, that
would have been a fine present—but
not to Patton. He wrote to Beatrice
while in the hospital, "Peace looks
possible, but I rather hope not for I
would like to have a few more fights."[2]

Hospital Can Wait

As Patton was rushed to
the hospital after being
shot in the leg, he made
a decision that could
be considered either
brave or foolish. On the
way, he insisted that the
ambulance driver stop at
division headquarters so
he could fill out his report
on the battle. Only after
the paperwork was com-
pleted did he resume his
trip to the hospital.

The War's Consequences

The armistice signed in November 1918 that officially ended World War I had greater implications that anyone could have imagined. The treaty punished Germany by taking away a large part of its territory and all but eliminating its armed forces. The German people grew angry over the armistice, and German political leader Adolf Hitler would later use their feelings to his advantage. He spoke often about how he would free Germany from the shackles of the agreement if given the chance. Because of that promise, Hitler was able to become dictator of Germany. He eventually launched World War II, which resulted in the deaths of at least 50 million people.

Patton would eventually have many more fights, but he would have to wait 25 years for them.

Patton as a colonel in World War I

Patton rejoined the cavalry after World War I.

TOUGH TIMES
BACK HOME

ollowing the war, the vast majority of
people and their national leaders had no
stomach for more. The war that had just ended was
termed "the war to end all wars"—at least, that was the
hope. But it was not the hope of Patton, who watched

as the U.S. War Department drastically decreased the size of his beloved tank corps. What had grown to 20,000 officers and enlisted personnel was cut, in 1919, to only 2,662.

Patton believed peace required a strong military to deter other nations from waging war. During the next two decades, he would warn of coming disaster as aggressive, maniacal leaders took over Germany, Japan, and Italy. He believed they would take advantage of the military weakness and the lack of desire to fight of the United States and European countries. He was eventually proven right.

After World War I, the U.S. Army had a policy of demoting soldiers to their prewar rank. This meant that Patton was demoted to the rank of captain. The next day, however, he was promoted to the permanent rank of major and remained as the commander of the 304th Tank Brigade. He realized that leading a downgraded tank corps during peacetime was not good for career advancement. So, Patton rejoined the cavalry. He was made commanding officer of the Third Cavalry at Fort Myer, Virginia. He went from teaching tank warfare to the more primitive duty of horse soldiering.

Carrying on the Family Name

Patton felt little joy about his professional life at the time, but a bundle of joy arrived on Christmas Eve in 1923. It was the son he had always wanted to carry on his name—George Smith Patton IV.

Patton's frequent moves continued in the 1920s. In 1924, he was assigned to the General Staff Corps in Boston, where he could spend more time with his family. But a year later, he was shipped out to the U.S. Army's Hawaiian Division in Honolulu. Here, he was put in charge of personnel and intelligence.

Like Father, Like Son

Many believed that Patton's son would follow in his father's footsteps. They were right. George Patton IV became a cadet at West Point during World War II, graduating in 1946. He spent the next 34 years in the army. Following the death of his father, he legally changed his name from George Patton IV to George Smith Patton.

The younger Patton became a company commander of U.S. troops during the Korean War in the early 1950s. He later served as a colonel during three tours of duty in the Vietnam War in the 1960s.

After the Vietnam War, he commanded the Second Armored Division at Fort Hood, Texas, the same unit his father had led during the North African campaign in World War II. Patton twice earned the Distinguished Service Cross, the army's second-highest award for combat heroism, and was eventually promoted to major general. Following his retirement in 1980, Patton moved to the family home in Massachusetts and became a farmer, raising blueberries and other produce. He named the fields on his farm after fallen soldiers whom he commanded in Vietnam.

He learned to enjoy the exotic location, playing polo every day and gaining friends among the wealthy. The Pattons were wealthy themselves, particularly after the death of Beatrice's father, Frederick, who left an inheritance of $20 million.

But the pursuit of financial reward did not drive Patton. Neither did the lifestyle of the rich. By 1926, he had become bored with anything less than military greatness. He wrote to Beatrice that he had "always hoped that as a result of a great war" he would "secure supreme command." After that war, he hoped he would "become President or dictator by the ballot or by force." But as no war appeared on the horizon, he feared he would be forced to retire "a useless soldier."[1]

However, if he was to be a useless soldier, he preferred to be one in Hawaii, and he asked permission to stay there. But in 1928, the U.S. War Department transferred him to the Office of the Chief of Cavalry in Washington DC. He soon embarked on rewriting the army manual on the pistol and reconsidering his philosophy on tank warfare.

Patton wrote papers downplaying the importance of tanks in future battles. He did so to remain loyal to his beloved cavalry, which some believed should be phased out in the new world of tank warfare. His written views often seemed to contradict those he had expressed during and after World War I. In one article, he claimed that tanks could not operate successfully in many different types of terrain. He added that the need for infantry and cavalry would not diminish in future conflicts:

> *I have flown, ridden and walked over every part of every place that I have been stationed ever since mechanization came up, and I have seldom found places where any machines could operate without the assistance of infantry to fight for it and cavalry to see for it.* [2]

Depressing Times

By the early 1930s, the thought of war was not foremost in the minds of U.S. citizens. The United States

Well-founded Fear

Though his feelings changed in the 1920s and 1930s, Patton's fear that an enemy would eventually use tanks to its advantage was well founded. The German army, under the guidance of Adolf Hitler, set out to maximize the potential of tanks. The devastating assault of a large number of fast tanks and bomber planes was unveiled in World War II. It became known as a *blitzkrieg*, or lightning war.

was gripped by the Great Depression. It was the worst economic calamity the country had ever experienced. The unemployment rate soared, long lines formed at soup kitchens every day, and many people became homeless.

In 1932, a group of World War I veterans became restless and angry. In 1924, Congress had promised that a lump sum of money would be available to them in 1945. But due to the financial distress, they wanted it right away. When Congress rejected their request, 17,000 veterans converged on Washington DC. Nicknamed the "Bonus Army" by the press, the former soldiers came to the nation's capitol to air their views, but their protest soon turned to violence.

President Herbert Hoover called on Douglas MacArthur to take steps to quell the Bonus Army riot. MacArthur turned to Patton. He arrived at the head of a cavalry

Purple Heart

In 1932, the Purple Heart, the military award honoring those injured during combat, was reestablished. That year, Patton was awarded the Purple Heart for being wounded in action during World War I.

Fame after the Bonus Army

Patton was not the only officer sent by General MacArthur to quell the Bonus Army protesters who would later gain greater fame. Major Dwight D. Eisenhower was also dispatched to the scene. Eisenhower would later distinguish himself as the commander of the European Allied forces in World War II. He also became a two-term president of the United States.

brigade of 217 men and 14 officers that were joined by infantry and several small tanks. The veterans were forced out, but not before several were killed and dozens wounded.

Aside from the Bonus Army fiasco, the Great Depression had not affected Patton. He was living the lifestyle of the wealthy. Still, Patton did not feel fulfilled. Only the excitement of war could do that.

George Smith Patton IV, left, followed in his father's military footsteps.

Japanese troops attacked China while Patton was in Hawaii in 1937.

PRELUDE TO WAR

In the spring of 1935, Patton was again transferred to Hawaii to work as an intelligence officer. He and his family remained in the U.S. territory of Hawaii until June 1937, when they sailed their own ship, the *Arcturus*, to

San Diego, California. By the time Patton returned
to the United States, the world was becoming a
far more dangerous place. Japan had conquered
Manchuria and had launched an invasion of China.
Italy had taken Ethiopia by force. Spain was being
torn apart by civil war. And, most ominously, the
ruthless dictator Adolf Hitler was openly preparing
for war.

Still on the Move

Patton was back in the saddle, commanding the
Fifth Cavalry Regiment at Fort Clark, Texas. But he
was soon transferred to Fort Myer, Virginia. The
previous commanding officer at Fort Myer had been
Colonel Jonathan Wainwright, who had gone broke
during the Great Depression. Since Fort Myer was
a showplace for the army, it required a commander
who had personal wealth and social breeding. Patton
was considered a far better choice than Wainwright.
Ironically, it was his wealth that doomed Patton to
this assignment, which he came to despise.

Patton was convinced that his previous position at
Fort Clark would have been much better for his army
career than his post at Fort Myer. But he was wrong.
The move brought Patton in contact with General

George C. Marshall, who would have a large role in the military during World War II and would prove helpful for Patton's career.

On September 1, 1939, German troops poured over the border into Poland, launching World War II. The German tactics proved that Patton and his original philosophy regarding tank warfare had been correct. For the first time in history, the Germans staged a massive assault using thousands of fast and extremely mobile tanks. The Polish military was taken by surprise. On the battlefield, the Polish cavalry attempted in vain to stem the tide of powerful German tanks.

In the summer of 1940, Patton

Meeting of the Minds

By the time World War II approached, Patton was again strongly advocating mechanized warfare. Several high-ranking army officers did likewise, including Adna Chaffee Jr. In the spring of 1940, Chaffee, Patton, and several others met in the basement of a Louisiana high school and organized a recommendation that the army create an independent armored force.

The recommendation was forwarded to General George C. Marshall, who quickly accepted it. He assigned Chaffee to command the new force. Chaffee, in turn, created the First and Second Armored Divisions and coordinated the use of armor, infantry, and artillery.

Though no record of the basement meeting was kept, it has been speculated that Patton played a key role in developing Chaffee's strategies. What is evident is that Chaffee gained a great deal of respect for Patton. This showed in Chaffee's appointment of Patton to commander of the entire Second Armored Division.

was given command of the Second Armored Division at Fort Benning, Georgia. By fall, he had been promoted to brigadier general. On April 4, 1941, he was promoted to major general.

War Closes In

Sensing an opportunity to once again lead troops in a time of war, Patton threw all his energy into his work. His primary focus was maximizing the speed and mobility of his armored forces. He studied ways to transform newly drafted recruits, who had not volunteered for service or ever wanted to join the army, into effective soldiers in a tank unit.

Though his knowledge of tank warfare proved beneficial, it was his personality and spirit that earned him the reputation as one of the finest trainers of soldiers in history. Despite self-doubts throughout the years, he instilled in his men a belief

"[Patton is] an outstanding leader who has great mental and physical energy. Because of his innate dash and great physical courage and endurance he is a cavalry officer from whom extraordinary feats might be expected in war."[1]

—Brigadier General Kenyon A. Joyce, Fort Clark base commander

German soldiers marched down a street in Poland
after the 1939 invasion of the country.

in themselves and their cause. Patton biographer

Alan Axelrod wrote:

> [Patton's] message was never we must succeed but always we
> will succeed. . . . When he spoke of combat, he spoke viscerally,

of blood and guts, but he also emphasized that blood and guts had to be mastered by intellect and put into the service of the great weapon they now possessed: the tank. [2]

Patton was ready for war, but the United States was not—even after Germany invaded France in June 1940 and staged nightly bombing raids over England. The United States was providing weapons for the British, but the majority of U.S. citizens still favored staying out of the conflict.

The events of December 7, 1941, changed that sentiment. On that day, Japanese planes roared overhead and bombed Pearl Harbor, Hawaii, killing nearly 2,400 people. After President Franklin Roosevelt's speech to Congress the next day, Congress declared war on Japan. Soon, Hitler lived up to his alliance with Japan by declaring war on the United States.

Efficient Troops

Military maneuvers called war games were meant to test the effectiveness of men, machines, and tactics under actual combat condition. During combat maneuvers in Tennessee in June 1941, Patton showed that he was ready to lead the Second Armored Division in war. The exercise was supposed to take two full days. Patton's troops were so efficient, they completed the operation in just nine hours.

The United States responded by declaring war on Germany, officially entering World War II in both Europe and Asia. Patton could not have been more ready to fight. ⌐

Patton oversaw U.S. troops in training exercises.

The U.S. Army Desert Training Center in California had similar conditions to North Africa, where Patton and his troops were going.

"Old Blood and Guts"

Following the bombing of Pearl Harbor, nearly all who had pleaded for the country to stay out of the war were now fervent about its involvement. U.S. citizens were banding together for a common cause.

Patton eagerly awaited his assignment, and he did not have to wait long. He was told to create and lead the U.S. Army Desert Training Center. He was greatly disappointed with this position. He craved action and had hoped to be sent into battle.

But Patton followed orders. In 1942, he surveyed the Mojave Desert, which covers parts of Arizona, Nevada, and California. Patton selected a location in California about 200 miles (322 km) east of Los Angeles for the training center. The mission was to prepare troops for combat in North Africa. The Allied forces, spearheaded by U.S. and British troops, planned to gain a foothold there. They hoped to use North Africa for an eventual invasion of Italy and France, which had been overrun by the Germans.

Patton's placement of the training center proved to be ideal for simulating the conditions in North Africa. It featured sand, cactus, rocks, snakes, and temperatures soaring to 130 degrees Fahrenheit (54°C) in the summer. He ordered that there be no electricity or running water. He wanted to test his tanks and his men. Patton and his trainees slept in tents rather than barracks and were forced to take eight-mile (13-km) marches every day.

He threw everything he had into his mission. From April through July he trained thousands of soldiers for combat while experimenting with various tank formations and strategies.

Throughout his months at the training center, Patton often pleaded with his superiors to send him overseas to fight. While they considered him a fine officer, they also believed him to be a remarkable trainer and the perfect commander in the development of U.S. tank warfare. He finally got his wish in July 1942. He received word that he would command the Western Task Force in the invasion of North Africa.

New Combat Vehicle

During his three months at the U.S. Army Desert Training Center in California in 1942, Patton did more than train troops. He also developed plans for an experimental new vehicle. It was a tank retriever, which was designed to recover damaged or broken-down tanks from the field under fire.

STILL BATTLING HIS DOUBTS

During his two-week voyage to Morocco, Patton had plenty of time to wrestle with his fears. He knew that he was about to face the challenges of battle command for which he had worked his entire life. He also knew that if he failed, many men would be needlessly killed. The freedom of the United States and the world depended greatly on him. Patton expressed the importance of his upcoming endeavor in a letter to his wife:

> *I think that one's spirit enlarges with responsibility. In 40 hours I will probably be in battle and on the spur of the moment with little information I will have to make most momentous decisions, and I feel that with God's help I shall make them right. It seems to me that almost in spite of myself my whole life has been pointed to this moment.*[1]

Morocco was a French colony, but France had been conquered by Germany. Nobody knew if the U.S. troops would be welcomed to the country or be shot at. On November 8, 1942, they found out. When U.S. warships headed toward the Moroccan port city of Casablanca, they were shot at. The U.S. troops fired back, and the naval battle began. Once Patton's men hit the beach, they started digging foxholes, or pits, where they could hide from incoming fire.

Patton saw these actions as cowardice. Instead of digging foxholes, the men should have been setting up stations and signal posts. Patton flew into a rage. He shouted and cursed at his men, even kicking one soldier to get him moving. But the opponents seemed to be in no mood to fight. With their fleet battered from the initial battle, they called for a cease-fire. Patton's planned assault on Casablanca proved unnecessary. The town quickly became a training base where new soldiers and equipment arrived from the United States.

But Patton wanted more battle, particularly in Tunisia, where the Allies needed assistance fighting the Germans. He was forced to restlessly wait for a call to action.

That call came in February 1943, soon after German troops attacked and drove back the Second U.S. Army Corps in northern Tunisia. U.S. troops had fought

The Biggest Enemy

The United States was lured into World War II by the Japanese attack on Pearl Harbor. Even so, President Franklin Roosevelt and U.S. military leaders thought that the defeat of Nazi Germany should be the top priority.

German dictator Adolf Hitler, who rose to power along with his brutal Nazi Party in 1933, sought war. In the late 1930s, French and British leaders were so eager to avoid conflict that they gave into all of Hitler's demands for land, including a large chunk of Czechoslovakia. Then Hitler's military took control of the rest of Czechoslovakia in 1939. The governments of England and France understood that Germany was not about to stop. They further realized that Germany had developed into a military giant when it destroyed Poland in a matter of weeks.

Germany's six-week conquest of France, completed in June 1940, sent shock waves throughout the free world. Many believed that Britain would also be forced to surrender as German planes began a nightly bombardment of its major cities. The defeat of Germany became even more important when reports circulated about its brutal treatment of people in the occupied countries.

poorly and retreated from the Germans. Although the unit managed to prevent the Germans from reaching a critical supply depot, the operation had still been a military catastrophe. The Second Corps lacked morale and discipline.

Patton to the Rescue

General Dwight D. Eisenhower, who was leading the theater of operations, knew quite well who could fix the problem. He called upon Patton, giving him just ten days to transform the corps into an elite and motivated fighting unit. Eisenhower commented, "For such a job, Patton has no superior in the Army."[2]

Patton whipped the sloppy, demoralized group into shape with a combination of tough discipline and acts of kindness. He forced all the men—even those who were not soldiers, such as doctors and cooks—to salute and wear helmets and proper uniforms at all times. Any soldier caught not acting or dressing like a soldier was given a heavy fine. Patton performed well enough in his duties to be promoted to lieutenant general.

In mid-March 1943, Patton led the newly trained Second Corps in an attack against German and

Italian troops in Tunisia. The Germans responded with a heavily armored counterattack, but they were stopped dead in their tracks.

Patton's philosophy was to always remain on the attack. He wanted to wedge his men between the Germans and the sea to cut off an escape route to Italy. But he was told to halt. The order confused and angered him. After all, he had the Germans reeling. Why, he asked, should he and his troops stop pushing?

The answer was that General Harold Alexander had convinced Eisenhower that his British Eighth Army, led by General Bernard Montgomery, could finish the job in Tunisia. Patton talked Eisenhower into keeping the Second Corps in the battle, but command of the unit was transferred to General Omar Bradley. Patton was assigned the task of directing the invasion of Sicily, an island off the coast of mainland Italy.

With this, Patton was one step closer to an invasion of Europe that would end the tyranny of Nazi Germany and achieve victory in World War II.

Patton watching his troops' movements in Tunisia

Patton delivered a talk to his troops before the invasion of Sicily.

FIGHTING HIS WAY
TO FRANCE

In 1943, the Allied strategy heading into the attack on Sicily was akin to a child's game of hopscotch. First they would attack Sicily, then mainland Italy, then France, then Belgium, and finally Germany. Patton published a message to the

90,000 men he was about to lead in the invasion of Sicily. It served as a pep talk before the critical fight:

> In landing operations, retreat is impossible. To surrender is as ignoble as it is foolish. . . . However tired and hungry you may be, the enemy will be more tired and more hungry—keep punching. No man is beaten until he thinks he is. . . . The glory of American arms, the honor of our country, the future of the whole world rests in your individual hands. See to it that you are worthy of this great trust.[1]

What Patton did not express to his men was his disappointment that the invasion of Sicily was to be spearheaded by Montgomery's British Eighth Army. His own troops would be used only as support. Patton was also irked that Eisenhower—a U.S. soldier—agreed to the plan. Patton would never forgive Montgomery and would spend the rest of the war trying to beat the British general to every battle destination.

Sicily Attack Planned

Allied leaders bickered for three months over a plan for the invasion of Sicily in 1943. The plan was completed in a bathroom at Allied headquarters in Morocco when Montgomery cornered Walter Bedell Smith, Eisenhower's chief of staff, at a sink. Montgomery breathed into an overhanging mirror. He then outlined a map of Sicily on the foggy glass. He traced where the various units would land and proceed. Because Montgomery had direct contact with British Prime Minister Winston Churchill, both Smith and Eisenhower lacked the courage to oppose the plan. It was then adopted.

True to form, Patton placed himself in grave danger during the Sicily campaign. The day after the attack began, he attempted to sneak between the Germans and the U.S. First Division in a jeep. Along the way, he dodged fire from snipers and tanks as well as fragments of U.S. anti-aircraft rounds that were aimed at German fighter planes.

Patton's handling of the Seventh Army led to a swift conquest of western Sicily in just a few days. The capital city of Palermo and 44,000 prisoners were captured. The speed of the takeover frightened the Italians, who feared an invasion of the rest of their country. They staged an overthrow of dictator Benito Mussolini, who was an ally of Hitler and the Germans.

Patton's Temper

The path to the city of Messina, Sicily, proved far more treacherous. German resistance stiffened, and Patton's drive was stopped cold. Frustrated and discouraged, he

Mussolini's End of Power

The overthrow of Italian dictator Benito Mussolini did not last long. In a daring rescue operation, the Germans helped Mussolini escape from prison and placed him back into power. At the end of the war, Mussolini tried to escape to Switzerland. But he was captured by angry Italians and hanged. His body was strung up in public to confirm his demise.

As lieutenant general, Patton led U.S. troops in the invasion of Sicily.

visited a U.S. evacuation hospital to talk with the wounded men. He tried pleasantly to cheer them up. As he was leaving, he noticed a soldier with no wounds. He asked the man what was wrong.

The man replied, "I guess I just can't take it," whereupon Patton slapped the man's face with his gloves and ordered him back into action.[2] Medical officers later diagnosed the soldier as suffering from dysentery and malaria.

One week later, as Patton still struggled to reach Messina, he visited another evacuation hospital. When a soldier admitted that he could not stand the shelling anymore, Patton struck the man, swore at him, accused him of cowardice, and even reached for his pistol. It became one of the most publicized and darkest moments of Patton's career. It was later discovered that the soldier was AWOL, or absent without leave. He had illegally left his unit and could have been court-martialed and shot, but this side of the story was never reported in the news.

Eisenhower ordered Patton to apologize to the soldier and the medical personnel and patients who had witnessed the incident. Patton also apologized in a note to Eisenhower, writing:

> *I am at a loss to find words with which to express my chagrin and grief at having given you, a man to whom I owe everything and for whom I would gladly lay down my life, cause for displeasure with me.* [3]

Eisenhower later explained to handpicked members of the media that the intensity and passion that motivated Patton to slap the soldier was also what made him a great army leader. The media members agreed to keep the incident a secret from the U.S. public, but it eventually found its way into a radio broadcast in Washington DC. Drew Pearson, a communist sympathizer, broadcast the story. Patton was criticized strongly by politicians, writers, broadcasters, and the public. But his superiors had too much admiration for his work to send him home.

Patton's Support

Though the slapping incident initially caused uproar, the vast majority of letters sent to Patton by U.S. citizens were quite complimentary. According to his aide, Colonel Charles Codman, nearly 90 percent of all the letters he collected indicated that the public supported Patton and understood his motives. Parents of sons who had served under Patton during the war had written some of the letters.

LEFT OUT OF THE OPERATION

Patton was punished, however. He was not allowed to participate in the invasion of Italy after Sicily had been secured. Patton feared his error would prevent him from commanding U.S. soldiers ever again.

But he did not need to worry. He was soon transferred to England to help plan the greatest military venture in history—the Allied invasion of Europe. Operation Overlord was intended to free the continent of German occupation and bring victory to the Allies.

Another Problem for Patton

The slapping incidents had faded into memory when Patton got into more trouble. But on this occasion, false media reports were to blame. While at a women's club meeting in Knutsford, England, Patton was persuaded to make a few comments. He told the women:

. . . since it is the evident destiny of the British and Americans and, of course, the Russians to rule the world, the better we know each other, the better job we will do.[4]

When the story was reported in the United States, Patton was misquoted. His quote excluded any mention of the Russians. A number of newspaper editors who disliked Patton took this chance to attack him. They claimed he had purposely offended Russia, an ally, by not mentioning the country as a world power.

Later media reports corrected the mistake and added Patton's inclusion of the Russians in his speech. But many still complained about the report. Once again, Patton's job was on the line. But Eisenhower believed the task at hand in France was far too important to risk by firing an able commander. He kept Patton as head of the Third Army.

Eisenhower became Supreme Commander of the Allied Expeditionary Force that would invade France on June 6, 1944. General Montgomery was to lead the British forces. Bradley was in command of the U.S. Twelfth Army. Though Patton was left in a subordinate role, he did not complain because of his respect for Bradley and his eagerness to return to battle. Patton was given command of the U.S. Third Army.

Patton was far from thrilled about the strategy for the attack, which was to be launched on the French shores of Normandy. He feared the troops would have difficulty advancing from the beachhead. The man whose military philosophy was "in case of doubt, attack" deemed it simply too timid.[5] He proposed that his Third Army land at Calais, France, which was closer to Germany, and drive directly toward the German capital city of Berlin. Patton insisted to Bradley that such a plan would maintain the offensive if the troops could not advance at Normandy. Bradley turned the matter over to Eisenhower, who dismissed Patton's idea.

Patton and his Third Army remained in training in England on D-Day, June 6, 1944. That was the

Staying Objective

Patton did his best to avoid becoming emotionally involved with the wounded he inspected at evacuation hospitals. He believed feeling sorry for them would discourage him from asking his own soldiers to risk their lives. He wrote in his diary on August 6, 1943: "One man had his head blown off, and they were just waiting for him to die. He was a horrid bloody mess and was not good to look at, or I might develop personal feelings about sending men to battle. That would be fatal for a General."[6]

day thousands of Allied troops risked their lives by landing on the coast of France. Many were killed by German fire as they emerged from their ships or set foot on the beach, but the operation was a success. Both the British and U.S. units established positions on French soil.

Soon it would be Patton's turn. Appropriately enough, he and his men set out for France on July 4, U.S. Independence Day. They were determined to rid the world of Nazi tyranny and help the people of Europe regain their independence. ⌒

Eisenhower, left, and Patton, right, discussing the war

Patton and other officers witnessed the burnt bodies of Holocaust victims at a German concentration camp.

Heroism and Tragedy

atton could hardly contain his eagerness as he awaited permission to enter the war in France. He was relocated from England to Normandy, France, in early July 1944. However, he was forced to wait a couple more weeks while

Allied units cut through the German defenses on
their way to Paris. When word arrived of a failed
July 20 assassination attempt on Hitler, Patton
became anxious that the war would end before he
would get another chance to fight. It had been 11
months since he had seen combat action.

Finally, on July 27, he was ordered to take
command of armored divisions of the Third Army.
The delay in joining the campaign benefited Patton.
The Germans had been pushed back, which gave his
tank units more room. At this point, mobile and
aggressive warfare was needed, and Patton was the
man to lead the charge.

He made his presence felt immediately. Patton's
troops swept through northern France. Within
three days, his troops had reached Avranche.
The following day, they captured the bridge at
Pontaubault, giving U.S troops pathways south, west,
and east to the Seine River and Paris.

Patton was just getting started, though. In only
two weeks, he led an advance through Normandy,
encircling thousands of German troops along the
way. His units liberated towns and villages from
Brest in western France to approximately 250 miles
(402 km) eastward. Patton would have liked to have

been the only commander in the area. He wrote to Beatrice: "We took Brittany, Nantes, Angers, LeMans and Alencon and several other places still secret. . . . I feel that if [I were] only unaided I could win this war."[1]

Patton, along with the members of his Third Army, experienced the joy of liberating Paris, which had been under German occupation for more than four years. Patton, however, had other goals besides Paris in mind. He wanted to be the first U.S. commander to invade Germany. He continued to head east with the goal of reaching Strasbourg on

Facing the Holocaust

The most chilling moments of many soldiers' experiences of war in Europe did not occur during battle. They took place when they came upon the extermination camps constructed by the Nazis. British, Russian, and U.S. troops liberated many of the camps in which millions of people were murdered. The majority of those killed were Jews, who Hitler and the Nazis deemed to be an enemy of Germany.

Patton visited the Ohrduf camp in late April 1944 and was appalled to see the thousands of bodies of murdered victims. He later said, "[It was] the first horror camp any of us had ever seen. It was the most appalling sight imaginable."[2]

Patton later visited a more notorious concentration camp in Germany called Buchenwald. A U.S. diplomat noted that Patton was so appalled during his time at Buchenwald that he "went off to a corner thoroughly sick."[3] The murder of the millions of people, particularly the Jews, in the extermination camps became known as the Holocaust.

the German border and, eventually, the coveted
Rhine River.

Ground to a Halt

By the end of August 1944, the Third Army
was only 100 miles (161 km) from the Rhine, but
they had to stop. The gasoline that should have
gone to Patton's Third Army was given to General
Montgomery. Montgomery's operation, however,
turned out to be a disaster and wasted time, material,
gasoline, and lives. Patton told Bradley he could be
in Germany within two days if his tanks could be
refueled, but he was ignored.

The gasoline shortage was accompanied by a
lack of general supplies, forcing Patton's race to
Germany to come to a halt. He was further frustrated
by a radio broadcast that claimed Eisenhower had
praised Montgomery as the greatest living soldier
and had promoted him to field marshal. Patton
knew that his Third Army had liberated most of
northern France and felt that Montgomery had done
very little. Eisenhower's remarks made Patton feel
unappreciated.

The weather became an enemy as well. Patton
was resupplied in September, but heavy rains slowed

his drive. His troops lost their momentum. As a result, the First Army, commanded by Courtney Hodges, crossed over the German border before him. Patton's troops met fierce resistance and moved slowly. A lack of supplies again stopped him in October.

By November, the Third Army had gained little ground and paid for every mile with blood. When Germany unleashed a surprise offensive in mid-December, thousands more U.S. lives were lost. The Third Army was in danger of being pushed back.

The Germans' attack in the thick, forested Ardennes region of Belgium stunned everyone except Patton. He had warned the headquarters of the Allied Expeditionary Force about the possibility of such an attack, but he had been ignored.

The Germans' push forward led to what became known as the Battle of the Bulge. Patton planned on sending in three divisions of his Third Army, most of which had been moving east toward Germany and now had to turn back west.

During a meeting of military leaders in mid-December, Patton claimed his men could launch a counterattack on December 22. Some of the British officers laughed, thinking it could never be done. This would require Patton's men to stop, turn around, march many miles in the ice and snow without rest, and attack to the north in only a few days. It was a feat that few other than Patton's army could accomplish, and it set off on the task.

The main task was to free Allied troops who had been surrounded by German troops in the Belgian town of Bastogne. Once the weather was better, air support was able to back the army with a massive bombardment. Patton's men liberated the town of Bastogne just as he had promised.

Patton and the Allied forces never again lost their momentum. The Battle of the Bulge was the last German offensive of the war. After that, Patton was forced to remain mostly on the defensive while Montgomery received permission from Eisenhower to resume the offensive into Germany. Patton was angry and frustrated at being forced out of the action. He also felt insulted that Eisenhower never praised him for his work in Bastogne. Bradley and Hodges received medals for their performance during the Battle of the

Wanting to Keep Fighting

Patton did not want his war to end when the guns went silent in Europe. He asked to be transferred to a command in Asia, where the United States was still fighting Japan. That would have placed Patton alongside famed U.S. General Douglas MacArthur. But Patton's request was turned down.

Bulge, but Eisenhower did not thank Patton for the difficult task he and his men had accomplished.

The Third Army closed in on the Rhine River in early February, but Eisenhower again asked Patton to take more of a defensive stand and give some of his troops to Montgomery for a stronger thrust into Germany. Patton replied to Eisenhower, through Bradley, that he would resign before he would stop his own offensive. Patton continued his strategy.

Mission Accomplished

Patton desperately wanted to beat Montgomery to the Rhine—and he did so on March 7, 1945. His advance through Germany included the capture of many towns and the virtual elimination of the German Seventh and First Armies.

The end of the war in Europe was now just a matter of time. Patton's Third Army rolled through southern Germany with less and less opposition. By the end of April, they had taken in more than 1 million prisoners, but Patton would not be allowed to continue to Berlin. He was disgusted to learn that the honor would be reserved for the Russians.

Patton and his men were sent to Czechoslovakia, where pockets of German resistance remained.

Thousands of people gathered at the Los Angeles Coliseum to welcome home U.S. soldiers.

On April 30, Hitler committed suicide. Then, on May 7, before the Third Army could liberate the country, Germany surrendered. The fighting in Europe had finally, and mercifully, ended.

In June, Patton returned home to a hero's welcome. Approximately 750,000 people cheered him along a parade route in Boston, Massachusetts, and 130,000 more shouted their praises at the Los

Angeles Coliseum. He then returned to Germany, which had become a U.S. occupation zone, where he would serve as an administrator of the area. He was planning to return to the United States on December 10, 1945, to celebrate Christmas with his family.

He never made it. On December 9, his chauffeured limousine crashed into an army truck in Germany. Patton was completely paralyzed. As he struggled to survive in the hospital, he uttered that losing his life in such a way would be "a hell of a way for a soldier to die."[4] After all, he had once said, "the only way for a soldier to die is by the last bullet in the last battle of his final war."[5]

Patton died on December 21, 1945, and was buried next to his fallen troops at a U.S. military cemetery in Hamm, Luxembourg. Thankfully he had not fallen in battle, because the war could not have been won without him. ⌐

The Troops' Success

Patton did not look in the mirror to find the hero of the campaign against Germany in World War II. Instead, he gave the credit to his soldiers. As he spoke to a group of 400 wounded men after the victory parade in Boston, he said, "With your blood and bonds, we crushed the Germans before they got [to the United States]. This ovation is not for me, George S. Patton— George S. Patton is simply a hook on which to hang the Third Army."[6]

A statue of Patton at the General Patton Memorial Museum
in Chiriaco Summit, California

TIMELINE

1885	1896	1903
George Smith Patton III is born in San Gabriel, California, on November 11.	Patton attends the Classical School for Boys.	Patton attends the Virginia Military Institute.

1912	1916	1918
Patton finishes fifth in the pentathlon event at the Summer Olympics in Stockholm, Sweden.	Patton accompanies General Pershing to Mexico in an attempt to hunt down Mexican bandit Pancho Villa.	Patton sees his first combat action as commander in World War I on September 12.

1904

Patton becomes a cadet at West Point Military Academy.

1909

Patton graduates forty-sixth in a class of 103 from West Point.

1910

Patton marries Beatrice Ayer in Massachusetts on May 26.

1918

Patton is shot in the thigh in combat on September 26.

1932

Patton heads an army group to quell the "Bonus Army" riot in Washington DC.

1934

Patton is transferred to Hawaii to serve as an intelligence officer in the U.S. Army.

TIMELINE

1935	1942	1943
Patton warns of a Japanese attack on Pearl Harbor. The harbor is attacked six years later in 1941.	Patton assumes command of the U.S. Desert Training Center in California.	Patton takes over the beleaguered Second U.S. Army Corps in Tunisia in February.

1944	1944	1945
In late August, Patton is within 100 miles (161 km) of the Rhine River in Germany with the Third Army.	On December 26, Patton's men begin a counterattack after the German offensive in the Battle of the Bulge.	On March 7, Patton and his men reach the Rhine River ahead of his British rival Field Marshall Bernard Montgomery.

1943	1943	1943
In March, Patton's troops play a major role in defeating Germans and Italians in North Africa.	Patton leads the Seventh Army in a successful Sicily campaign.	On August 3, Patton slaps a soldier; it nearly ends his career.

1945	1945	1945
On May 7, Germany surrenders, removing the need for Patton's Third Army to liberate Czechoslovakia.	Patton is paralyzed when his chauffeur-driven limousine crashes into an army truck on December 9.	On December 21, Patton dies from injuries suffered in the accident.

Essential Facts

Date of Birth

November 11, 1885

Place of Birth

San Gabriel, California

Date of Death

December 21, 1945

Parents

George Patton II and Ruth Wilson

Education

Classical School for Boys; Virginia Military Institute; West Point Military Academy

Marriage

Beatrice Ayer (May 26, 1910)

Children

Beatrice Jr. (1911), Ruth Ellen (1915), George IV (1923)

Career Highlights

George S. Patton is one of the most recognized generals of World War II. During that war, he led successful campaigns in North Africa and Europe that contributed to Germany's defeat and the Allies' victory.

Societal Contribution

Patton foresaw the necessity for the U.S. Army to incorporate tank warfare into its military strategy. Because of this, the Allies were able to competitively fight German troops on land during World War II.

Conflicts

In 1943, Patton slapped an officer, causing Patton to be rebuked by higher army officers and personal humiliation. Patton was repeatedly ignored in his military opinions, including his warning of a potential attack on Hawaii and his requests to be further involved in battle.

Quote

"In landing operations, retreat is impossible. To surrender is as ignoble as it is foolish. . . . However tired and hungry you may be, the enemy will be more tired and hungry—keep punching. No man is beaten until he thinks he is. The glory of American arms, the honor of our country, the future of the whole world rests in your individual hands. See to it that you are worthy of this great trust."
—*George S. Patton, 1943*

Additional Resources

Select Bibliography

Axelrod, Alan. *Patton: A Biography*. New York, NY: Palgrave Macmillan, 2006.

Blumenson, Martin. *The Patton Papers: 1885–1940*. Boston, MA: Houghton Mifflin, 1972.

Blumenson, Martin. *The Patton Papers: 1940–1945*. Boston, MA: Houghton Mifflin, 1972.

D'Este, Carlo. *Patton: A Genius for War*. New York, NY: HarperCollins, 1995.

Patton, George S. Jr. *War as I Knew It*. Boston, MA: Houghton Mifflin, 1995.

Peifer, Charles Jr. *Soldier of Destiny: A Biography of George Patton*. Minneapolis, MN: Dillon Press, 1989.

Further Reading

Hatch, Alden. *Old Blood and Guts*. New York, NY: Sterling Publishing, 2006.

Hirshson, Stanley P. *General Patton: A Soldier's Life*. New York, NY: HarperCollins, 2002.

Hymel, Kevin. *Patton's Photographs: War as He Saw it*. Dulles, VA: Potomac Books, 2006.

Web Links

To learn more about George S. Patton, visit ABDO Publishing Company online at **www.abdopublishing.com**. Web sites about George S. Patton are featured on our Book Links page. These links are routinely monitored and updated to provide the most current information available.

Places To Visit

General George Patton Museum
4554 Fayette Avenue, Fort Knox, KY, 40121
502-624-3812
www.generalpatton.org
Learn about the life and career of Patton at a museum officially dedicated on May 30, 1949, by his widow, Beatrice.

National World War I Museum
100 West Twenty-sixth Street, Kansas City, MO, 64108
816-784-1918
www.theworldwar.org/s/110/index.aspx
Learn more about what was supposed to be "the war to end all wars"—the first war in which Patton fought.

National World War II Museum
945 Magazine Street, New Orleans, LA, 70130
504-527-6012
www.ddaymuseum.org/
Find out more about World War II and the D-Day invasion at this museum.

GLOSSARY

adjutant
A military officer who assists a commanding officer.

Allies
Nations fighting on the same side as the United States during World War II; these include the United States, the United Kingdom, France, the Soviet Union, and China.

artillery
Equipment that fires guns or rockets long distances.

bombardment
The act of dropping bombs out of fighter planes.

cadet
A student at a military school.

captain
Army rank above lieutenant and below major.

cavalry
Part of a military force that serves on horseback.

colonel
Army rank above major and below general.

Confederate
A supporter of the South during the Civil War.

corporal
Army rank above private and below sergeant.

counterattack
A military offensive to counter one made by the enemy.

evacuation hospital
A military hospital where wounded soldiers are treated.

general
> Highest army rank; the army has five levels of general.

liberate
> To free a country controlled by force by another country.

mettle
> Courage.

occupation
> The control by force of one country by another.

offensive
> A military attack.

orderly
> A soldier who performs tasks, such as carrying messages, for an officer.

salient
> A line of defense that is farther outward than the rest of the line, projecting into enemy territory.

shelling
> Artillery fire.

sniper
> A hidden gunman attempting to shoot and kill enemy soldiers.

tank
> An armored combat vehicle equipped with weaponry.

West Point
> Home of the U.S. Military Academy.

Source Notes

Chapter 1. Broken Leg, Damaged Spirit

1. Stanley P. Hirshson. *General Patton: A Soldier's Life*. New York, NY: HarperCollins, 2002. 217.
2. Frederick Ayer Jr. *Before the Colors Fade: Portrait of a Soldier, George S. Patton, Jr.* Boston, MA: Houghton Mifflin, 1964. 104.
3. Martin Blumenson. *The Patton Papers: 1885–1940*. Boston, MA: Houghton Mifflin, 1972. 916.
4. Ibid. 915–916.
5. Frederick Ayer Jr. *Before the Colors Fade: Portrait of a Soldier, George S. Patton, Jr.* Boston, MA: Houghton Mifflin, 1964. 105.

Chapter 2. A Young Soldier

1. Stanley P. Hirshson. *General Patton: A Soldier's Life*. New York, NY: HarperCollins, 2002. 20.
2. Martin Blumenson. *Patton: The Man Behind the Legend, 1885–1945*, New York, NY: William Morrow, 1985. 24.
3. Mostafa Rejai and Kay Phillips. *World Military Leaders: A Collective and Comparative Analysis*. Santa Barbara, CA: Greenwood Publishing Group, 1996. 59.
4. Stanley P. Hirshson. *General Patton: A Soldier's Life*. New York, NY: HarperCollins, 2002. 23.
5. Carlo D'Este. *Patton: A Genius for War*. New York, NY: HarperCollins, 1995. 64.
6. Ibid. 249.

Chapter 3. School and Love

1. Martin Blumenson. *The Patton Papers: 1885–1940*. Boston, MA: Houghton Mifflin, 1972. 84.
2. Carlo D'Este. *Patton: A Genius for War*. New York, NY: HarperCollins, 1995. 77.
3. Martin Blumenson. *The Patton Papers: 1885–1940*. Boston, MA: Houghton Mifflin, 1972. 185.

Chapter 4. First Tastes of Battle

1. George Forty. *The Armies of George S. Patton*. London, UK: Arms and Armour, 1996. 16.
2. George S. Patton Jr. *War as I Knew It*. Boston, MA: Houghton Mifflin, 1995. xvii.
3. Army Times. *Warrior: The Story of General George S. Patton, Jr.* New York, NY: G. P. Putnam's Sons, 1967. 44.
4. Stanley P. Hirshson. *General Patton: A Soldier's Life*. New York, NY: HarperCollins, 2002. 123.

Chapter 5. Combat in World War I

1. Carlo D'Este. *Patton: A Genius for War*. New York, NY: HarperCollins, 1995. 243.
2. Martin Blumenson. *Patton: The Man Behind the Legend, 1885–1945*. New York, NY: William Morrow, 1985. 114.

Chapter 6. Tough Times Back Home

1. Stanley P. Hirshson. *General Patton: A Soldier's Life*. New York, NY: HarperCollins, 2002. 188.
2. Ibid. 195.

Chapter 7. Prelude to War

1. Martin Blumenson. *The Patton Papers: 1885–1940*. Boston, MA: Houghton Mifflin, 1972. 931.
2. Alan Axelrod. *Patton: A Biography*. New York, NY: Palgrave Macmillan, 2006. 77–78.

Chapter 8. "Old Blood and Guts"

1. Martin Blumenson. *The Patton Papers: 1940–1945*, Boston, MA: Houghton Mifflin. 1972. 99–100.
2. Charles Peifer Jr. *Soldier of Destiny: A Biography of George Patton*, Minneapolis, MN: Dillon Press, 1989. 76.

SOURCE NOTES CONTINUED

Chapter 9. Fighting His Way to France
1. Martin Blumenson. *The Patton Papers: 1940–1945*. Boston: Houghton Mifflin, 1972. 274–275.
2. Stanley P. Hirshson. *General Patton: A Soldier's Life*. New York, NY: HarperCollins, 2002. 389.
3. Carlo D'Este. *Patton: A Genius for War*. New York, NY: HarperCollins, 1995. 543.
4. Stanley P. Hirshson. *General Patton: A Soldier's Life*. New York, NY: HarperCollins, 2002. 460.
5. Robert H. Patton. *The Pattons: A Personal History of an American Family*. Dulles, VA: Potomac Books, 2004. 151.
6. Alan Axelrod. *Patton: A Biography*. New York, NY: Palgrave Macmillan, 2006. 115.

Chapter 10. Heroism and Tragedy
1. Martin Blumenson. *The Patton Papers: 1940–1945*. Boston: Houghton Mifflin, 1972. 512.
2. George S. Patton Jr. *War as I Knew It*. Boston: Houghton Mifflin, 1995. 292.
3. Alan Axelrod. *Patton: A Biography*. New York, NY: Palgrave Macmillan, 2006. 161.
4. Martin Blumenson. *The Patton Papers: 1940–1945*. Boston: Houghton Mifflin, 1972. 512.
5. Frederick Ayer Jr. *Before the Colors Fade: Portrait of a Soldier, George S. Patton, Jr.* Boston: Houghton Mifflin, 1964. 1.
6. Martin Blumenson. *The Patton Papers: 1940–1945*, Boston: Houghton Mifflin, 1972. 721.

Index

INDEX CONTINUED

ABOUT THE AUTHOR

Martin Gitlin was a reporter for two newspapers in northeast Ohio for 20 years before becoming solely a freelance writer. During his two decades as a reporter, Gitlin won more than 45 awards, including first place for general excellence from the Associated Press in 1995. The Associated Press also named him one of the top four feature writers in the state of Ohio in 2001. Gitlin has written more than a dozen educational books about sports and history.

PHOTO CREDITS